Francis of Assisi

Life and Brief Devotions

Francis of Assisi

Life and Brief Devotions

by Jeffrey Keefe, OFM Conv.

Illustrations by
Berard Hofmann, OFM Conv.

BOOKS & MEDIA

BOSTON

Imprimi Potest:
    Francis Edic, OFM, Conv.
    Minister Provincial

Nihil Obstat:
    Bede Babo, OSB
    Censor Librorum

Imprimatur:
    † James A. McNulty
    Bishop of Paterson

Revised 1993 Edition

Original Title: *Singer, Soldier, Saint*

Printed and published in the U.S.A. by Pauline Books & Media, 50 Saint Pauls Avenue, Boston MA 02130-3491.

www.pauline.org

Pauline Books & Media is the publishing house of the Daughters of St. Paul, an international congregation of women religious serving the Church with the communications media.

7 8 9 10 11 12 13   07 06 05 04 03 02

Francis of Assisi is the world's most popular saint. Not a year passes without the appearance of new books about him, each author attempting to present some original slant on this charismatic man. More biographies have been written of St. Francis than of any other saint. These books have not been written only by Catholics. Some fine works have come from the pens of Protestants. One famous treatise had an atheist as its author. St. Francis' electric personality and mystical character have entranced the whole world for eight centuries.

Pope Leo XIII called St. Francis the most perfect imitator of Christ. A generation ago, an apostle of youth, Father Daniel Lord, S.J., labeled St. Francis the most Christlike saint. Indeed, as though to stress the resemblance of Francis to the Master, God visibly impressed the five wounds of the passion on this singing saint. Yet, though Francis imitated and reflected the Lord so well, Francis remained his own unique self.

St. Francis was born in 1182. His father, Peter Bernardone, was rather well-to-do. He belonged to the new class of merchants who had become rich on the trade boom following the Crusades. Bernardone was an importer and dealer in cloth in the town of Assisi in north central Italy. If Francis were alive today, his family would be upper middle class, in the two-home and three-car bracket.

Formula for a Favorite

Twin traits account for Francis' popularity with his boyhood friends. And these same traits Francis developed to become the great saint he is. They are characteristics rather common to most boys, though Francis had them in an uncommon degree. The beguiling twosome which made Francis so magnetic to his companions, and to the people of the eight centuries which have passed since he was a teenager, were cheerfulness and generosity.

Though he had at least one brother, Francis was his father's favorite. Peter liked to hear Francis' cheerful songs around the house and shop. The boy was very fond of French, the native tongue of his mother. He sang in French so often that his father called him "Francesco," which in Italian simply meant "Frenchy." Actually, his baptismal name

was John. It's rather appropriate that such a jaunty fellow as Francis should be honored in heaven by his nickname.

Whenever any celebration was going on in town, Francis would not only be in the thick of it, but usually led the fun. Baton in hand and garland on brow, he would be acclaimed king of revelry. Often he led his careless and carefree companions through the streets singing and shouting, a practice some of the older citizens of Assisi did not appreciate, especially after bedtime.

Yet, Francis knew good times need not interfere with the commandments. He was respectful, especially toward men and women of the Church. His companions were well aware that their "king" would not tolerate any indecent antics or jests. In later life, Francis' struggle for purity was a very human feature of what otherwise might have seemed a too-easy virtue. But Francis had laid the strong foundation for this virtue during his teenage search for values.

As well as being naturally cheerful, Francis was big-hearted. Among his friends he was known as a free spender. Even when it didn't mean having a good time, Francis was generous. One day while he was tending his father's store, a tramp came in and asked in Christ's name for a handout. Francis was busy with a customer, and brusquely showed the derelict the door. As soon as he realized what he had done, he ran out, leaving his surprised customer fingering a bolt of cloth. When he overtook the beggar, Francis emptied all the coins from his pockets into the poor man's hands.

Only the Best

Francis' father was not reluctant to give Francis anything he wanted. He bought him the best clothes and added a liberal allowance. Peter Bernardone was proud when his customers and business associates would remark: "Your Francesco is quite a boy. He'll make the Bernardone name famous some day."

The Francis who approached manhood was merry, impulsive, generous, somewhat spoiled; he was the leader of the heedless, noisy partygoers of the town. Francis went through his teen years in high spirits. And yet there was an undertone of serious thought. He pondered what he would do with his life. He could easily take over his father's cloth trade; it offered security and a position among the city's powerful merchants.

But Francis simply did not have the temperament or the talent to be a businessman. Francis, though a magnetic leader, was neither an organizer nor an administrator. Later in life, when a religious Order mushroomed around him, one of the Cardinals befriended him and took care of most of the details of organization for him.

Francis' romantic spirit was captivated by the ideal of knighthood. Today's counterpart might be a young boy's dream of entering a service academy, although the knights of the thirteenth century had much more glamour than the military of today. The knights were the defenders of right and virtue. They were chivalrous gentlemen, noble men of honor and integrity, the heroes of every tale and tune.

A skirmish between Assisi and a neighboring city gave Francis his first chance for manly combat. He went off to the war against the neighboring town of Perugia, full of the enthusiasm that sparks those who are no longer boys and not yet men. His career ended quickly; he was taken prisoner and jailed for a whole year. During this period he was the "life of the jail," as he had been the "life of the party" back home. He kept the morale of the prisoners high despite the poor food and filthy cells and unnerving idleness. In fact, the other p.o.w.s began to suspect that Francis must be crazy because he was so cheerful when there was really nothing to be cheerful about.

Finally the Assisians were released. Home again, Francis fell seriously ill. Probably the long confinement had weakened his health. After he recovered he did not seem to be his old self. He still led the merrymakers of Assisi, but he was losing his taste for that sort of pastime. His friends teased him, saying that he must be in love.

He decided to try the knightly career once more. His father was all for the idea. He had noticed that Francis was uneasy; maybe a campaign would recapture the cheerful lad he had been before.

Peter Bernardone arranged for Francis to enter the corps of the local duke, who was preparing for service in the south. He bought Francis a fine horse with all the trappings of the warrior: coat of mail, tempered sword and handsome lance. Francis rode off with banners flying.

Knight Without Armor

On the following night the band of warriors camped out. Francis slept soundly, and in a dream a voice asked him, "Francis, is it better to serve the master or the servant?" Francis gave the obvious answer, "Why, the master, of course." The voice retorted, "Then why do you make a master of the servant?"

Francis awoke troubled. Somehow knighthood suddenly had lost its luster. He had entered, more deeply than most, a common crisis of young men: indecision regarding vocation. Next morning he turned his steed northward and returned home.

Imagine the reception he got. The gallant knight-to-be had returned after a career of two days! His father, who had bragged about his son, was forced to listen to the snickers and jokes aimed at the boy.

As if this humiliation were not enough to bear, Peter Bernardone observed that Francis was now moody. The extrovert had become more reserved. He shunned night life and spent too much time (thought the senior Bernardone) in St. Damian's Chapel outside the city walls.

One day Francis was pacing his horse, trying to think through his future. He passed a leper pleading for alms. Naturally Francis dreaded coming into contact with lepers, pitiable and frightful as they were, covered with sores and rotting flesh. Lepers were repulsive; no one contested that. But they were all the more ghastly to Francis since he was something of a dude.

He threw a coin at the poor fellow and tried to pass him by. But in a flash, Francis fathomed the cause of his unsettled moods. Any Christian could toss a coin at a leper; but he himself, he now saw, was the type who could not be satisfied with the minimum; he was not made for halfway measures. The impulsive horseman leaped to the ground and threw his arms around the fetid, foul-fleshed leper as though the miserable man were his best friend

whom he had not seen for years. And in truth Francis did see his best friend in the leper; he saw his brother in Christ.

In the months which followed, Francis moved toward greater peace of soul. One day, while he was praying in St. Damian's Chapel, the figure on the cross spoke to him: "Francis, restore my Church, which you see falling into ruins."

Francis took the words at face value. Indeed, St. Damian's was in rough shape. The walls were cracked, the stucco peeling, the roof let in jagged streams of light—and sometimes streams of water.

Francis returned to his father's shop and helped himself to some of the best velvets and Eastern brocades. He sold the cloth in nearby Foligno and offered the money to the priest of St. Damian's. But the priest, even though he knew that Francis came from a wealthy family, was reluctant to accept the gift. He did not know what to make of this "convert"; perhaps this was his idea of a practical joke.

The bag of coins suddenly had become a bother to Francis, so he flung it on a windowsill of the church in case the priest should change his mind.

When Signor Bernardone learned what had occurred, he completely lost his long-seething temper. This incident was the last straw. He hunted Francis out, grabbed him by the collar, hauled him to the bishop's palace, and demanded his money back. The bishop saw Peter Bernardone's point, and told Francis he had no right to give away his father's money without permission.

The money was recovered, for the priest had not touched it. Francis was so shocked at his father's concern about a little money when he had so much, that he returned not only the money but everything his father had given him, including the clothes he wore. The bishop provided him with a peasant's smock, on which Francis chalked a cross. Unique in everything, Francis even reversed the role of father disowning son. He said to the bishop, "Now I can say, 'Our Father who art in heaven.'"

Francis now divided his time between doing his chores in a leper hospital and repairing St. Damian's Church with his own hands. He made the rounds in Assisi asking for stones to finish this task. He even begged from his old friends, the same young men and women whom he used to lead in revelry. Francis' own brother publicly ridiculed him. Children taunted him in the streets.

Seeing all this, Francis' father was beside himself with anger and shame. Actually, Peter Bernardone must not be blamed too severely. He simply did not realize—nor did anyone, even Francis—the peculiar path to greatness God had planned for Francis.

In early youth Francis had hoped to gain acclaim and applause as a knight. How many people today, if any, could name a single knight of St. Francis' day? Yet few living today have not heard of the saint of Assisi.

The Spontaneous Order

Francis was happy helping the priest and the lepers, owning only the clothes he wore. Yet he was not entirely satisfied; he knew by some mysterious sense that he still had not found his niche in life. Daily he attended Mass. Daily he prayed that God would make his vocation clear.

His answer finally came on the feast of St. Matthias, February 24, 1209, when he was about twenty-six years old. As the priest read the Gospel, Francis was struck by the words: "Provide yourself with neither gold nor silver nor copper in your belts: no traveling bag, no change of shirt, no sandals, no walking staff. The workman, after all, is worth his keep" (Mt. 10:9f.). After Mass Francis rushed to the sacristy and asked the priest to explain this passage. The priest told him that the Apostles were directed by the Savior to be unconcerned about earthly goods so as to give their full attention to preaching the Gospel. As the priest developed this theme for his young helper, Francis' eyes glowed with enthusiasm and he exclaimed, "That is what I wish to do; that is what I desire and seek with all my heart."

Francis took these words of the Gospel as the blueprint for his life. In them he perceived a summary of Christ's life. The Savior did not concern Himself about worldly goods. He chose poverty and journeyed about preaching the kingdom of God.

With the bishop's permission Francis now began to preach simple sermons to the townsfolk. His mode of life had already met with a great deal of scoffing. A converted pleasure seeker was one thing; it was quite another now that he took to preaching. Nevertheless, some men of Assisi were impressed by the young socialite who had given himself so completely to the pattern of Christlike character.

One such gentleman was Bernard of Quintavalle. Like Francis' father, Bernard was an astute merchant. But like Francis, he found much of the behavior of the wealthy class a sham. A cautious and practical man, before he made any definite decision about Francis he wanted to test whether he was dealing with a fanatic or a faker. So he invited Francis to spend the night at his home. After they had dined and talked a long time, Bernard brought Francis to his own room where he had a second bed.

They retired and Bernard pretended to doze off. At last Francis, thinking his host asleep, got out of bed and knelt in ardent prayer throughout the night. Bernard then knew that Francis was a sincere and holy man. He asked if he might join him in his way of life.

Immediately afterward, a second prominent citizen, Peter of Cataneo, made the same request. Peter was also a successful man, a brilliant attorney.

God Points a Finger

Francis realized that he must have some specific plan for the spiritual life. With characteristic trust in God, he led Bernard and Peter to St. Nicholas' Church, took the missal from the altar, and opened it at random three times. The first time his finger hit this text: "If you seek perfection, go, sell your possessions and give to the poor. You will then have treasure in heaven" (Mt. 19:21).

The second words were the same which had struck Francis so forcibly when he first heard them, the text that told him to take nothing for the journey.

The final words he pointed to were another passage in St. Matthew's Gospel. "If a man wishes to come after me, he must deny his very self, take up his cross and begin to follow in my footsteps" (Mt. 16:24).

Francis adopted these three directives, stressing the virtue of poverty, detachment from the world's goods, and penance, as the core of his rule of life and the outline of Franciscan spirituality.

He advised Bernard and Peter to give their wealth to the poor. His new followers did this gladly; they believed that they had the better of the bargain in exchanging the worry and responsibility of property and money for the freedom to follow Christ without concern for any other goal in life.

Soon other men followed the example of Bernard and Peter. Francis, who always insisted on obedience to the Church authorities, wanted to get permission for the Order which he saw forming without any conscious effort of his own. When the band of Poor Men had grown to twelve, they set out for Rome to seek an audience with Pope Innocent III. It was the year 1209.

The Pope Is Surprised

The night before Francis was to present his plea, Pope Innocent had a strange dream. He dreamed that the Church of St. John Lateran, which is the cathedral church of the Pope, was on the verge of crumbling into ruins. Just as the edifice was about to collapse, a small man appeared, stretched his arms in the form of a

cross against the facade of St. John's, and by this support prevented it from destruction.

The next morning Pope Innocent went through the routine business of the day: appointments with cardinals and nuncios and ambassadors. He was weary after a troubled night and thankfully approached the last scheduled audience. This was with some unknown from Umbria who had been recommended by Cardinal Hugolino. But the Pontiff's fatigue vanished when the man in peasant garb entered the hall; Innocent recognized Francis as the little man of his dream.

The Pope interpreted the dream as a sign from God that Francis was destined to save the Church from ruin. For at this time in history, it was threatened on two fronts: by crafty rulers trying to make the Church a department of State, and by a careless clergy not sufficiently dedicated to the spiritual welfare of the people. Pope Innocent freely gave Francis permission to follow his Gospel mode of life and to establish a company which would imitate the complete poverty of Christ and preach simple, straightforward sermons to the faithful.

Thus it was that the Franciscan Order officially began, founded not by any design of Francis, but by the will of God, who used him as a magnet to draw generous men to the imitation of Christ.

The Franciscan Apostolate

Once papal approval was gained, the original twelve friars returned to the vicinity of Francis' home town. They lived together

in a stable, a stone hovel called Rivo Torto—
"twisted river" in Italian—because a stream
wound past the site. Rivo Torto was the first
home of the Franciscan Order. Here Francis
spent his happiest and most peaceful days.
Here he and his friars lived the ideal Gospel
life without any of the feverish dissensions
which later infected the Order.

While at Rivo Torto, the friars' life was one
of prayer, work and preaching. At first Francis
preached on street corners or market squares.
Then pastors asked him to their churches. His
sermons were so moving that the local canons
invited him to speak in the cathedral.

Francis began, or perhaps revived, a new
style of preaching. He insisted that sermons
be for the edification and benefit of the people
in their everyday language. He even urged in
the Franciscan rule of life that sermons be
brief, because this was the manner of our
Lord's talks. Francis made no attempt to
impress his hearers with learning or oratory.
His appeals were marked by conviction and
sincerity. He spoke of the love of God, the
mercy of Christ, the grace of the Holy Spirit.
As a result, Franciscan preaching has always
had the trademark of simplicity, stressing the
basic truths of the Catholic Faith.

Sermon Equipment

When Francis went to a church for a preaching assignment he often appeared with, of all things, a broom. This may seem eccentric, but Francis was moved by such deep faith and great love for our Lord in the Eucharist that he could not bear to see an untidy church. Unfortunately, in Francis' day, some pastors did not care properly for their churches. Francis rightly thought that churches should be immaculate, however poor, and he was willing to clean them himself. After he had finished the job, he would speak to the pastor privately and remind him of his obligation to Jesus present in the Blessed Sacrament.

Some time later, when Francis took over the direction of the nuns of St. Clare, one of the main works he assigned them was making altar linens. The Poor Clares donated these linens to impoverished priests so everything connected with the altar would be respectable and spotless.

Life at Rivo Torto was rugged. As more friars joined Francis, the decrepit stable became overcrowded. Francis solved his housing problem with a piece of chalk. He marked off a space for each friar. When, finally, there were more friars than spaces, Francis assigned each brother a shift for sleeping.

ing. Guy was rich and his hospitality more than matched his wealth. When Francis and his companions arrived at Guy's mansion, the rich young man would not allow the servants to wait on the friars; he insisted on doing so himself. He washed the friars' feet after their journey and personally served them at meals. The gracious host told the brothers that they should consider his house as their own. Francis was so charmed by this courtesy that he asked his friars to pray that God would give Guy the grace of a vocation to their fraternity. Guy proved to be as generous with God as he was courteous with others. Unlike the rich young man in the Gospels, he responded to his vocation and became a Franciscan. Courtesy had won a liberal thank-you from God.

The Same Francesco

As Francis prospered in the serious business of becoming a saint, he did not lose his natural quality of cheerfulness. On one occasion when the going was particularly rough at Rivo Torto, his followers were rather discouraged. Always a mimic, Francis grabbed a couple of sticks, and with a few appropriate gestures transformed them into a fiddle and bow. He danced around, played his "fiddle," and sang until he managed to turn up the turned-down corners of his friars' mouths. Francis once declared, "It is for the devil and his members to be sad, but for us always to be cheerful and happy in the Lord." He used to say that there was only one excuse for a long face and that was mortal sin.

Francis kept his sense of humor too, and sometimes employed it to correct erring brothers. One young man had joined the ranks but did not show much enthusiasm at doing his share of the work; however this slack friar was a model of promptness at mealtime. Francis dubbed him "Brother Fly."

Nor did Francis become less generous as he became more spiritual-minded. He continued to give away everything in order to follow Jesus more perfectly. He had given up his fine home and his secure future. Now he gave his whole self, body and soul, to the service of Christ. When he had nothing to satisfy those who requested alms, he would give away his only tunic.

The point is, of course, that becoming a saint did not change Francis' personality. Rather, this project polished and perfected it, as following Christ does for anyone who dedicates himself entirely to this challenging goal. Such is actually the vocation of each human being. God does not expect everyone to be

another St. Francis or St. Clare. He expects
each one to be himself, to become St. Jim
or St. Jane or St. Whoever-one-happens-to-be.

The friars did not stay in Rivo Torto long. It
became smaller as the ranks grew larger.
Finally a peasant appeared and claimed the
place for a stable. Rather than argue the
point, Francis decided to leave. He meant to
own nothing, and therefore would not contest
the peasant's claim. The bishop of Assisi had

no place to offer the friars, but luckily the Benedictine abbot of Mount Subiaso gave St. Francis the nearby Chapel of Our Lady of the Angels. This place is called Portiuncula, or "Little Portion." It came to be the dearest of all to the heart of Francis. But since he wanted to live in absolute poverty he would not accept the chapel outright. He agreed to rent it from the abbot. Every year, until the Benedictine monastery was destroyed, the friars paid a basket of fish to the monks as their annual rent.

The Second Order

Francis' way of life attracted more and more people. Among them, the most generous yearned to follow his way of life completely, offering their lives to God's service and giving full attention to the salvation of their souls. One such person was Clare Scifi, a beautiful member of Assisi's upper class.

Clare knew her family would oppose her vocation, as Francis' father had opposed his. So she took only one of her aunts into her confidence and decided to leave home secretly and go to a convent. On Palm Sunday, 1212, Clare stole away to Portiuncula, where she was invested in her habit by St. Francis. He took her to live with the Benedictine Sisters in the neighboring Convent of St. Paul.

Clare's family was furious. Her father and brothers went to the convent to induce her to return home; but after much discussion they realized she was a strong-willed individual and finally surrendered.

However, two weeks later Clare's sister Agnes followed her. This time the family sent an armed troop to raid the convent and bring Agnes home by force if need be. The men tried to carry her off bodily. As legend has it, the slight young girl became so heavy that the men could not budge her. Frustrated, they gave up in her case as well. The hand of God was too evident. Both Clare and Agnes became canonized saints.

Clare wanted to found a community of nuns following the same rule of life as Francis' friars. Once again the Benedictine monks came to the rescue, donating the Church of St. Damian to Francis for Clare and her nuns. St. Damian's became the nursery of the Second Order of St. Francis, the Poor Clare nuns.

Operation: World

Meantime, Francis and his friars began to go beyond Assisi on their preaching tours. Francis did not intend to limit his preaching to the people of one town. He did not want to limit it in any way. He eagerly desired to preach even to the Moslems. Francis was the first founder of a religious Order to emphasize the mission apostolate in his rule. He encouraged missioners to the Saracens and other infidels, but kept such work on a volunteer basis.

Francis set out for Syria in the fall of 1212 in the hope of expounding the Gospel to the followers of Mohammed who controlled the Holy Land. But his ship sank in a storm off the coast of Slavonia, and he found himself stranded in a strange land with empty pockets (if he had pockets at all). He begged for return passage to Italy, but without success. Finally a sailor gathered some provisions and smuggled Francis and his companion friar aboard his ship. This vessel, too, met with a storm and was tossed off its course, making the journey longer than usual. As a result the ship's store ran low. The "stowaways" were discovered, and since there was a food shortage, Francis shared his little rations as best he could. This liberal gesture won the hearts of the crew. Instead of converting Saracens, Francis preached to sailors, and persuaded many lax crewmen to return to the sacraments once they reached shore.

The failure of his missionary adventure caused Francis to wonder whether perhaps God wanted him to become a contemplative, that is, to spend his life in prayer alone, rather than in an active ministry. He felt attracted to such a life of prayer ever since his absorbing days at St. Damian's. He asked God for guidance in making his decision and sent one of his friars, Brother Masseo, to learn the opinion of Sister Clare, and of Brother Sylvester, the first priest to join the Order. Brother Masseo returned with an identical response from each: Francis was to continue in the active apostolate of preaching.

Within a year Francis embarked once more to attempt to convert the Moslems. This time he traveled toward Morocco but fell sick in Spain. Francis considered this second mission failure as God's way of saying that he should return to Italy and manage his growing fraternity.

Yet these events crystallized the two main purposes of the Friars Minor, the "lesser brethren" as Francis called his followers. The friars were to preach the great truths of theology in the language of the ordinary person. And they were to announce the good news of the Gospels to souls in mission lands.

Francis' Difficult Years

Francis still had an overwhelming desire to be a missionary and a martyr. Five of his friars had won martyrs' crowns in Morocco. Others had established successful missions in eastern Europe and Syria. Francis had set out twice to preach to the Moslems. He had gone eastward but was defeated by storms at sea. He had trekked westward toward Morocco but was halted by illness. He decided that his third attempt would be to the south.

Francis traveled to Egypt, where a Crusade was in full force. As it turned out, this venture was no more successful than his previous ones, but it raised the curtain on one of the most colorful episodes in the life of the impetuous saint.

Francis, accompanied by Peter of Cataneo, the second man to join his fraternity, and a few other friars, landed at St. Jean d'Acre in July of 1219. The friars journeyed to Damietta, on the east branch of the Nile. Though under siege, the city was enjoying a temporary truce.

Francis had his own plan of attack, one which was completely oblivious of caution. He had come to preach to the Moslems. He decided that the simplest way to do this was to walk calmly to the enemy lines and begin. So before the astonished crusaders could keep

him from what seemed suicide, he chose a companion and strolled across the sandy waste toward the Moslem camp. His partner, Brother Illuminato, from all accounts, was not as calm as Francis, so Francis began singing a song to bolster his courage.

The Saracens were more surprised than the crusaders when they saw the two men in unusual costume approaching their encampment singing they knew not what. Pouncing on the friars, they began to maltreat them. Francis quit singing and began to shout, "Sultan, Sultan!" Not one to worry about protocol, he wanted to talk directly to the head man. The Saracens were so flabbergasted (and probably also a bit worried) when Francis cried "Sultan!" that they escorted him to their chief, Malek-el-Kamel.

The Sultan was enchanted by Francis' sparkling personality. He listened with courteous attention to his preaching about Christ the Redeemer; moreover, he gave Francis permission to preach to his subjects. But Christianity did not find appreciative ears among the Moslem Arabs, so the Sultan decided his guest had better leave before one of his scimitar-toting clansmen was overcome with religious zeal.

The Sultan graciously gave Francis a parting gift—a silver and ivory horn which the saint later used to call his hearers for sermons in the market squares. Then the ruler ordered an escort for Francis' return to the crusaders' camp. Francis retraced his steps, once again disappointed that his effort was not successful, and that he was still a live friar rather than a dead martyr. The Christian soldiers were amazed to see him and his companion again, particularly with their heads still securely attached to their necks.

Francis' Cross Takes Shape

Since he saw God's hand in the most ordinary events in life, Francis was now convinced that he was not destined to be a missionary, even though his Order was to become one of the largest missionary communities of the Church. Francis returned to Italy for years which were the hardest and most trying of his life. His eyesight began to fail, probably because of Egyptian eye sickness contracted on this last journey. A heavy burden for anyone, this was all the more severe for Francis, who was so sensitive to the beauty of nature. In September of the following year, 1220, he resigned as head of the Order because of his poor health, and gave the reins of authority to Brother Peter.

Unfortunately, Peter died the following March. Francis, of course, knew that Peter had gained heaven, but his death caused Francis deep natural sadness. Peter had been one of his very first disciples; often he had been Francis' vicar; more often, his companion.

Francis then chose Brother Elias to head the Order. Elias was a most capable man, but one wholly lacking Francis' sanguine temperament. Elias was practical; Francis was idealistic. Elias was an organizer; Francis would leave everything to Providence. Elias saw a need to introduce practices which Francis felt were not in keeping with a literal application of the Gospels.

Neither was wrong, really. The growth of the Order to include thousands of friars made some organization necessary; but the family-like quality of early years was lost. This was the great cross of Francis' life—the disappointment that, apart from its first idyllic days at Rivo Torto and Portiuncula, the brotherhood did not wholly achieve the ideals he had set for it. Part of this disappointment was due to Francis' own humility; he did not realize that his own life was too perfect for literal imitation. Part was due to the fact that Francis himself was not an organizer or administrator. Since he lacked a natural talent for such work, it necessarily fell to well-intentioned men who were better administrators than he, but whom he surpassed in the supernatural talent of completely following the poverty of Christ. In consequence, as Elias and the Church authorities made revisions in the pattern of the Order, Francis was deeply saddened because he felt the changes were not in keeping with the simple way of life outlined in the Gospel accounts.

Yet it was Francis and his Cardinal-friend who had chosen Brother Elias for this task.

Indeed, Francis chose Elias as his successor from thousands of friars, and even ahead of the survivors of the original dozen brothers who were so dear to him. And though Francis did not understand or agree, he humbly respected the authority to which he subjected himself. Nevertheless these developments made him heartsore and, added to his physical suffering, made these years the most grievous of his life.

Francis' Gift to Christmas

However, one event of these years has captured the heart of the Christian world. It took place near the village of Greccio at Christmas of 1223. A rich landowner, John Vellita, had given the friars the use of a wooded area for their retreats. A cave was on this property, and Francis conceived the idea that the celebration of the friars' Christmas should be at this cave to recapture the atmosphere of the first Christmas. He asked the landlord to arrange a manger in the cave and to bring a donkey and an ox so it would be like the stable where our Savior was born. The kind benefactor arranged everything in detail, and an altar was set up over the manger.

Francis was deacon of the solemn Mass. Present in the congregation, John Vellita saw something that he scarcely could believe. He saw an Infant lying in the manger, although it did not seem to move. Then Francis took the Babe in his arms and the mysterious Child stroked the saint's greying beard with his tiny hand. Since that Christmas scene took place at Greccio, Christians have copied Francis' touching tableau, and a manger scene has become part of the celebration of what Francis always referred to as "the feast of feasts."

The Third Order: Catalyst for Character

The reputation of Francis grew as the years passed. The daring feat of complete Gospel living made him something of a national hero. His friars numbered over five thousand. The nuns of St. Clare prospered with many vocations.

Francis' radicalism was almost too successful. Requests for admission to his Order even came from married persons who wanted to break up their homes and families in order to become Franciscans. These were not isolated cases. He received enough such petitions to make him realize that his movement, if unguided, might disrupt society by damaging family life. Just prior to and during Francis' own lifetime, other "returning-to-the-Gospel" trends had begun admirably, but turned heretical to plague the Church.

No one would have been more astonished than Francis to be called a genius. But his solution to this problem was one of the strokes of genius in his life. He had already revolutionized religious life. His fraternity transported religious life from the monastery to the parish church. Now his Third Order would bring friary and convent to the parish home.

Francis wrote a modified rule of life which could be kept by lay persons while retaining their state in life. It was designed for everyone, married or single, who desired to be more than average Christians. The rule established the Third Order of Francis,* a genuine, full-fledged Order, but without vows, and not binding under sin except in matters already covered by the commandments. The Third Order rule is built around moderation and penance; it is the catalyst for making the good better and the better saints. It is a transformer of Christian homes into sanctified homes, and has been called by Pope Leo XIII "my plan for social reform."

---

*In 1978 the Third Order adopted the new name, Secular Franciscan.

In growth, the Third Order dwarfed even the First and Second Orders. The henchmen of Frederick II, the emperor of the time, complained that their paganizing programs were defeated because there was a Franciscan tertiary in every family.

Suffering, Song and Sainthood

The new year, 1224, brought a minor improvement in Francis' health. By mid-year he felt well enough to undertake a retreat. He journeyed to La Verna, the mountain which the rich Duke Orlando of Cataneo had entrusted to him some years before. The nobleman had built a chapel on the wooded mountainside, and when Francis and his companions arrived, put himself at their disposal.

In August Francis began a fast which was to last from the Assumption to the feast of St. Michael, which falls in late September. Francis' natural joyfulness was still blighted by anxiety because his Order was not accepting his ideas as wholeheartedly as he had hoped. In order to revive his good spirits, he commissioned Brother Leo to open the Gospels haphazardly and read whatever text he lighted upon. Leo did this three times, and each passage concerned the passion of Christ. From this, Francis understood that his own passion had arrived, and that he must suffer this trial to the end. Brother Leo's action was a more literal prophecy, however, than either suspected at the time.

The Prophecy Fulfilled

Francis withdrew from the other friars. He ordered Leo to come to him twice a day with bread and water, and to make a third visit that they might recite the breviary prayers together. But before he crossed the bridge which spanned the gully separating Francis from the friars, Leo was directed to shout the first words of the divine office. If Francis answered the prayer, Leo could come across the bridge; otherwise, he must return to the other friars and leave Francis to his private devotions.

One night Francis did not answer the prayer. Leo's curiosity overcame his obedience. He crossed the footbridge and found Francis absorbed in prayer, lying face to the ground, his arms spread in the form of a cross.

The feast of the Holy Cross, September 14, increased the fervor of Francis' retreat. He had great devotion to the cross; the passion and the Eucharist were the focal points of his spiritual life. It had been the cross in the church of St. Damian which marked the begin-

ning of his new life when the figure on it spoke and urged him to rebuild the Church.

Meditating on the crucifixion, Francis prayed through the early morning hours. From the core of his soul he uttered this prayer:

"O Lord Jesus Christ, two favors I beg of Thee before I die. The first is that I may, as far as it is possible, feel in my soul and in my body the suffering which Thou, O gentle Jesus, sustained in Thy bitter passion. And the second favor is that I, as far as it is possible, may receive into my heart that excessive charity by which Thou, the Son of God, wast inflamed, and which moved Thee willingly to suffer so much for us sinners."

As Francis prayed for the pain of Christ and the love of Christ, an angel appeared, a seraph with six radiant wings, bearing an image of the crucified Savior. The vision told Francis that he would not be martyred as he so ardently desired. But he would be transformed into the likeness of Jesus by an inner flame. When the vision ended, Francis was left with the wounds of Christ reproduced in his own flesh.

From this moment all traces of dejection left him. Although his physical sufferings became terribly severe, he was completely at peace, a peace surpassing even his former cheerfulness. Francis did his best to keep the wounds from the gaze of his friars, but his blood-stained clothing revealed the secret.

Duke Orlando gave him a donkey to ride because the wounds on his feet made walking any distance impossible. As he left La Verna the news of the divine favor spread, and crowds formed in every town.

Francis returned to his beloved Portiuncula, which, after Rivo Torto, was the cradle of the Order. Despite his impaired health, and now the wounds of the passion, he seemed to have more energy than ever. He undertook all sorts of new endeavors. He made the rounds of the leper hospitals in the vicinity and helped the friars care for these poor unfortunates with their great open sores and ulcerous flesh. Some cases were so bad that maggots already infested the decaying sores.

One leper cared for by the friars had a bad disposition. Instead of appreciating the care of the friars, he complained and abused them. Francis took charge of this poor man and began to wash his sores, the stench of which the leper himself bemoaned he could not tolerate. He was already half-rotted before death. As Francis washed the piteous man, his flesh became whole again wherever Francis' hand passed over it, until he was entirely cured. The patient realized a miracle had happened to him. His joy gave way to shame and he begged pardon of the friars for his ingratitude toward their charity.

The Saint's Song

Elias became genuinely concerned over Francis' health. He never had been robust;

even when young he had been susceptible to fevers. Rigorous fasts and penances had drained his stamina; he now suffered hemorrhages of the stomach. His eyesight was completely gone at times. The wounds of Christ, blessing though they were, were another pain to be borne by his already weakened constitution. Even sleep was denied him, if not by his ills, then by field mice which ran over him while he lay in his hut at night.

It might be expected that anyone experiencing even some of this physical and nervous strain would give way to depression. Yet Francis was increasingly cheerful. In this tumult of suffering he reached an apex of joy, bursting forth with a serene song which is a masterpiece of world literature: his Canticle of the Sun.

The Canticle is a surging poem, called by one of the great biographers of St. Francis, "a symphony of all creatures...from cherubim to atoms." It reveals the intense degree to which Francis had received the Holy Spirit's gift of knowledge, the gift which aids a soul to see God reflected in His creatures, and creatures in their relation to God. Francis had a love of nature which was perfected supernaturally by this gift of the Holy Spirit. This perfection of Francis' natural temperament by sanctifying grace has given the world its most spiritual piece of literature apart from Scripture itself. Francis wrote his poem in medieval Italian, the tongue that needs no music to be melodius.

The urging of Elias and other friars moved Francis to go to the town of Rieti, where the Pope was at the time. There Francis could consult the papal doctors. The thirteenth century was poor in medical knowledge, and the doctors attempted to cure Francis' blindness by burning his temples with red-hot irons. This "cure" only increased Francis' grave physical suffering.

Next the friars brought Francis to Siena, which is famous for its healthful climate. But Francis knew he was dying and wanted to return to Assisi for his last days on earth. Brother Elias realized his case was hopeless and felt that he might as well comply with the dying saint's last wishes.

On arrival in Assisi Francis discovered that the bishop and the civil officials were in serious conflict. He asked both parties to assemble in the city plaza. There he assigned two friars to sing his Canticle, to which the peacemaker added four lines for the occasion, praising God on account of those who are willing to forgive for love of Him. These last lines so affected his hearers that all admitted their faults and forgave one another, restoring peace and good feeling to the city.

Francis knew that he would not live much longer. In September he asked his doctor to tell him the truth. The doctor, evidently an experienced practitioner, told Francis that he would live to the end of the month, or perhaps would last into early October.

Francis lay silent for a moment, then threw his arms outward and exclaimed, "Welcome, Sister Death!" With the close of his earthly life announced to him, he completed his great poem; he added the final spontaneous stanza in praise of God, who does not allow death to harm anyone who had done His will during life.

As September drew to a close, Francis' joy became greater daily. He asked Brother Angelus and Brother Leo to sing his Canticle to him over and over. He was so high-spirited that the strait-laced Elias worried over whether it might be a bad example for the people to hear a Friar Minor approaching death with so much merriment. But nothing could suppress Francis' cheerful confidence at meeting God, to whom he had never refused anything during his lifetime.

During these last weeks, Francis wrote his "will." This last testament was a plea to his friars, those living and those to come, to keep faithfully the vows and rules to which they pledged themselves.

Francis wanted to die at Portiuncula, the first permanent chapel and friary of his fraternity. His friars carried him there on a stretcher. Outside the city of Assisi they stopped and supported him, so he could look up and bless his native town.

Francis lay in a hut at Portiuncula for a week. Leo and Angelus repeatedly sang his song to him, and each time Francis sang the final verse praising the Lord for Sister Death. On Friday, October 2, 1226, he asked to be brought into the Chapel of Our Lady of the Angels and laid on the floor. Toward evening of the next day he blended his own voice with the voices of the singing friars. But this time he did not sing the last stanza of his Canticle; instead he began to chant the 142nd Psalm in a clear, strong voice: "Bring my soul out of this prison and then I shall praise your name. Around me the just will assemble because of your goodness to me." Finishing this last verse, he was silent.

As darkness shrouded the chapel, Francis entered eternal light.

Prayers to St. Francis of Assisi

Begging God's Gifts and Thanking Him

By choice and vow St. Francis was the "beggar saint," and before God we are all beggars who need divine aid. St. Francis knew that you must ask with faith if you wish to receive, and will help you to do so.

Above all, St. Francis is the saint of gratitude for the favors God gives us, and will help us imitate him by making our sense of thanksgiving manifest.

We invoke the aid of St. Francis of Assisi because in his time and place he was a perfect mirror of Christ, our Lord.

PRAYERS

St. Francis of Assisi, help us. By your example may we learn that life does not consist in the pursuit of wealth nor in the abundance of our possessions.

St. Francis of Assisi, come to our aid. Because we live at a time when men glorify ease and seek after luxuries, and when many wish only the gratification of fleshly desires, we stand in special need of your singleminded dedication to Christ in the narrow way that leads to life.

St. Francis of Assisi, assist us now. May we appreciate as you did the beauties of God's wonderful creation, and the glory of the world He made for us. Help us to enjoy and appreciate God's bounty without spoiling or defacing His gifts by our heedlessness and greed.

Teach us, seraphic Father Francis, to value all things as Christ did and to be imitators of Him as you were. May we thus enjoy the good things of life, but always prefer the blessings of the endless life to come. Amen.

V. God forbid that I should glory—

R. Save in the cross of our Lord, Jesus Christ.

St. Francis, the little poor man of Assisi, we invoke you as the admirable mirror you were of our Divine Master.

You imitated Christ the Lord in your humility and obedience. You faithfully followed Him in poverty and weakness. With joy you accepted suffering, contempt, and trials for the sake of His name.

In your goodness help us, then, to imitate your example. By your power with God obtain for us the special favor we now seek through your intercession.

Please pray for us, gentle and happy saint of the poor, that we may always be loyal followers of our Savior, Jesus Christ, and filled always with divine riches. Amen.

Prayer of St. Francis

LORD,

make me an instrument of Your
PEACE

where there is hatred let me sow
LOVE

where there is injury
PARDON

where there is doubt
FAITH

where there is despair
HOPE

where there is darkness
LIGHT

and where there is sadness,
JOY

O Divine Master,
grant that I may not so much seek to be con-
soled as to console; to be understood as to
understand; to be loved as to love; for it is in
giving that we receive, it is in pardoning that
we are pardoned, and it is in dying that we are
born to eternal life.

The Testament Prayer

We adore you, Lord Jesus Christ, in all Your churches in the whole world, and we bless You, because by Your holy cross You have redeemed the world.

Prayer Before the Crucifix

Most high, glorious God, enlighten the darkness of my heart. Instill in me a correct faith, a certain hope and a perfect love; a sense and a knowledge, Lord, so that I may do Your holy and true command.

Song of St. Francis

Since God is love,
  I'll sing His song.
With God above
  I will be strong.
With God within,
  What else need I?
While God shall reign
  Can my song die?

      —*Attributed to*
      St. Francis of Assisi

A Friar's Prayer

May my life of prayer and service, O Lord, show those I serve the reality of Your love. Make me poor, chaste, and holy that I may be an example to all who cross my path. May everything I do tell others I am happy serving them; may my life be a sign to your people, especially to the young who so carefully observe me, of the joy that should be mine in my vocation. Use me and my work, O Lord, that I may be the means of bringing fervent vocations to my Franciscan family. Amen.

**Conventual Franciscans
Vocation Office
St. Anthony on Hudson
Rensselaer, N.Y. 12144
Phone: (518) 436-8680**

BOOKS & MEDIA

The Daughters of St. Paul operate book and media centers at
the following addresses. Visit, call or write the one nearest you
today, or find us on the World Wide Web, www.pauline.org

CALIFORNIA
3908 Sepulveda Blvd, Culver City, CA
90230   310-397-8676
3945 Balboa Avenue, San Diego, CA
92111   858-565-9181
46 Geary Street, San Francisco, CA
94108   415-781-5180

FLORIDA
145 S.W. 107th Avenue, Miami, FL
33174   305-559-6715

HAWAII
1143 Bishop Street, Honolulu, HI
96813   808-521-2731
Neighbor Islands call:
800-259-8463

ILLINOIS
172 North Michigan Avenue, Chicago,
IL 60601   312-346-4228

LOUISIANA
4403 Veterans Memorial Blvd,
Metairie, LA 70006   504-887-7631

MASSACHUSETTS
Rte. 1, 885 Providence Hwy, Dedham,
MA 02026   781-326-5385

MISSOURI
9804 Watson Road, St. Louis, MO
63126   314-965-3512

NEW JERSEY
561 U.S. Route 1, Wick Plaza,
Edison, NJ 08817   732-572-1200

NEW YORK
150 East 52nd Street, New York, NY
10022   212-754-1110
78 Fort Place, Staten Island, NY
10301   718-447-5071

OHIO
2105 Ontario Street, Cleveland, OH
44115   216-621-9427

PENNSYLVANIA
9171-A Roosevelt Blvd, Philadelphia,
PA 19114   215-676-9494

SOUTH CAROLINA
243 King Street, Charleston, SC
29401   843-577-0175

TENNESSEE
4811 Poplar Avenue, Memphis, TN
38117   901-761-2987

TEXAS
114 Main Plaza, San Antonio, TX
78205   210-224-8101

VIRGINIA
1025 King Street, Alexandria, VA
22314   703-549-3806

CANADA
3022 Dufferin Street, Toronto,
Ontario, Canada M6B 3T5
416-781-9131
1155 Yonge Street, Toronto,
Ontario, Canada M4T 1W2
416-934-3440

¡También somos su fuente para libros, videos y música en español!

BOOKS & MEDIA

$1.95

ISBN 0-8198-6935-X

£1·50

9 780819 869357